CAMPUS JIHAD:

The Struggle Within The American University

NICOLE ANDERSON COBB, PHD

ISBN: 978-1-4834-3462-9 (sc)
ISBN: 978-1-4834-3461-2 (e)

Lulu Publishing Services rev. date: 9/15/2015

Set on a large state school campus at a fictional university, "Campus Jihad" chronicles the lives of a group of students, faculty, staff, administrators and community members negotiating their normal academic duties---while also struggling to manage their relationships with each other. As the semester begins, the environment is tense as issues of race and faith threaten to boil over.

On this campus, we meet the following characters: Craig, an African American undergraduate advisor and law student who works to help undergraduates with course advising, academic support and mentoring. Talib, is a Pakistani-American student Craig inherits as a part of this year's student assignments. Angel is a Cuban-Muslima and Craig's fellow law student. Bilal, is an African American Muslim undergraduate student and roommate of Talib. Hanna is a white female student and new convert to Islam in the local community. Dr. Evers is a sociology professor of Talib.

CHARACTER LIST

*(***) INDICATES THAT THESE INDIVIDUALS CAN BE DOUBLE CAST, TAPED BY OTHER ACTORS OR DOES NOT REQUIRE AN INDIVIDUAL TO BE PRESENT. ***ALSO, FOOTAGE OF THE PRESIDENT OBAMA SPEECHES CAN BE FOR THIS PRODUCTION.*

***PRESIDENT BARACK OBAMA: VOICEOVER

---TALIB: A SOUTHASIAN MALE, TEENS/EARLY 20s

---CRAIG: AN AFRICAN AMERICAN MALE, LATE 20s

---ANGEL: A LATINA FEMALE, MID-TO-LATE 20s

---HANNA: A WHITE, FEMALE WITH BLOND HAIR, BLUISH/ GREEN EYES, LATE TEENS EARLY 20s

---BILAL : AN AFRICAN AMERICAN MALE, LATE TEENS/ EARLY 20s

---MARTY: A WHITE MALE, LATE EARLY 20s, MUSCULAR BUILD

---CHRIS: A WHITE MALE, EARLY 20s, MUSCULAR BUILD

***IMAM HAKIM: VOICEOVER

***JONATHAN: VOICEOVER

---DR. EVERS: A WHITE FEMALE, 40-45

LIST OF ACTS AND SCENES

ACT I: 4 scenes
ACT II: 5 scenes
Act III: 6 SCENES

ACT I/OPENING SCENE

(THE SCENE OPENS WITH FOOTAGE OF
PRESIDENT BARACK OBAMA AS SEGMENTS OF
HIS CAIRO SPEECH OPEN THE SCENE.)

REMARKS BY THE PRESIDENT

ON A NEW BEGINNING

Cairo University

Cairo, Egypt

1:10 P.M. (Local)

President Obama: Thank you very much. Good afternoon. I am honored to be in the timeless city of Cairo and to be hosted by two remarkable institutions. And I am also proud to carry with me the good will of the American people, and a greeting of peace from Muslim communities in my country: Assalaamu Alaykum. (Applause).

I've come here to Cairo to seek a new beginning between the United States and Muslims around the world, one based on mutual interest and mutual respect, and one based upon the truth that America and Islam are not exclusive and need not be in competition. Instead, they overlap, and share common principles -- principles of justice and progress; tolerance and the dignity of all human beings....

The Holy Koran tells us: "O mankind! We have created you male and a female; and we have made you into nations and tribes so that you may know one another."

The Talmud tells us: "The whole of the Torah is for the purpose of promoting peace."

The Holy Bible tells us: "Blessed are the peacemakers, for they shall be called sons of God." (Applause.)

The people of the world can live together in peace. We know that is God's vision. Now that must be our work here on Earth.

Thank you. And may God's peace be upon you. Thank you very much. Thank you. (Applause.)

END

2:05 P.M. (Local)

###

(IN THE HALLWAY LOOKING FOR THE OFFICE NUMBER, A BROWN-SKINNED STUDENT OF SOUTH-ASIAN HERITAGE ENTERS, NERVOUSLY, WEARING JEANS, A UNIVERSITY HOODIE, AND BASEBALL CAP. HE REMOVES HIS CAP UPON ENTERING THE OFFICE AND RUNS HIS HANDS THROUGH HIS HAIR. TALIB GREW UP BETWEEN TWO WORLDS: HIS PAKISTANI FAMILY ENCLAVE AND WORKING IN HIS FATHERS' GAS STATIONS IN THE INNER CITY.)

TALIB
Mr. Brown, I'm Talib Husseini.
(TALIB holding a paper in his hand)

I got this form saying that you are my advisor this year.

CRAIG
(CRAIG Shaking hands with TALIB)
Yes, Talib. Come on in. And please, man, call me Craig.

TALIB
I've seen you at prayer sometimes at the mosque. Some of the other brothers have said that you are a great advisor....
they say they can really talk to you when they come by.

CRAIG
(CRAIG looking up from his folder and smiles, a bit embarrassed)
Well, that's very kind of them. I try to do my best for the students I work with. So, you are a Liberal Studies Major, huh?

TALIB
(TALIB, a little spooked at the question)
Yeah, I know it's odd. An Asian in the Humanities, right?
I know it goes against the stereotype: Muslims don't read. We're usually science and numbers guys.

CRAIG
(Noting his defensiveness)
Uh, no,…that's not what I was going to say at all. What I
was going to say is that few students do as well as you have
in courses with Professor Evers, who teaches Sociology or
Professor Simons, Euro-American Traditions course.

TALIB
Yeah, well, they were tough, but I was motivated…

CRAIG
By what?

TALIB
To learn about the West.

CRAIG
Why? (Smiling) Aren't you from Glenview? Isn't that part of "the West"?

TALIB
Please…that ain't the West, man?! That's suburbia.

(Both men laugh)

TALIB (CONT'D)
Besides, I'm really interested in Anglo-Islamic relations… I was
hyped to hear President Obama's speech in Cairo this past summer
about a new directions for US relations with the Muslim world.

CRAIG
So it sounds like you might be leaning toward
Humanities and International Relations?

TALIB
No, I love Humanities, but I keep up with the politics for my health.

CRAIG

What do you mean ...for your health?

TALIB

Anything going on in the Muslim world is bound to affect
my day-to-day--- so I try to keep tabs on things.

CRAIG

How is the President's speech in Cairo going
to affect your day -to-day, Talib?

TALIB

Because we catch it...WE Muslims live the "War On Terror" every day.

CRAIG

(CRAIG shaking his head trying to absorb Talib's words)
I feel you, man, I feel you. So, OK, let's get back on track.
So, you are pretty sure you want to do Humanities?

TALIB

(Sighs deeply)
Yeah, I guess.

CRAIG

Are you sure you don't want to CONSIDER at least
a minor in International Relations or Global Studies.
I think you'd be really good in these fields.

TALIB

(Getting a bit flustered)
Man, like I said, that's just for my survival, not for a school major?!

CRAIG

But I think you could really make an impact
perhaps be a bridge between....

TALIB

(A bit perturbed and loud)

Craig, man, did you hear me? I don't want to do it.

CRAIG

Listen, I'm just trying to find a good fit for you....

TALIB

(Frustrated)

Why? At the end of the day all you need to do is check the boxes, right?

CRAIG

Listen, I'm tryin' to help you pick the major that will be best for you and that will serve you and the issues you really care about.

(TALIB fidgets in his chair, adjusts his hat and looks at the floor.)

TALIB

Yeah, yeah, I know you're just trying to help me…it's just that …

CRAIG

What?

TALIB

(Shaking his head and mumbling under his breath)

It's fucked up.

CRAIG

What is?

TALIB

Just things!

CRAIG

Like what?

TALIB
(Laughing nervously)
Again with all the questions?

CRAIG
Talib man, is something wrong? You seem frustrated,
irritated… and the semester is just beginning?!

(Long quiet pause between the two men.)

TALIB
Can I talk straight to you?

CRAIG
(Closing his folder and dropping his pen)
Sure you can. That's why I'm here.

(Talib looks Craig in the eye with a curious expression.)

TALIB
…YOU ever get TIRED of pretending?… Ever get tired of ALWAYS
having to worry about whether folks are comfortable around you?

(The two men look into each other's eyes. Long pause.)

CRAIG
Yeah, sometimes I do.

(Talib gets up and turns around)

TALIB
I mean, I'm here in school, taking classes, being a "good"
student, trying to make my family proud especially since
my dad runs gas stations…but it's never enough.

CRAIG
For who, Talib?

TALIB
For the professors, for the police, the guys on the floor, it's
always some shit. One day it's "Hey Osama", next day, it's a flat
tire on my car or a derogatory note on my room door.

(CRAIG'S phone rings. TALIB squirms restlessly.)

CRAIG
(Answering the phone)
Hello, Craig Davis.

(CRAIG holding his hand over the phone)

CRAIG
Talib, this is my boss on the line. If you can wait, it will just be a moment.

(Back to phone)
Uh-huh…uh-huh…yeah, OK… I'm in with a student… When?…
TODAY?…What time?…4:00…OK, OK, see you then.

(Craig hangs up phone)

CRAIG
Sorry about that. Now you were talking about notes on your door? Who's
leaving these notes? Have you talked to your Resident Director about this?

(TALIB'S phone rings with the ringtone "Transformer" from Chris
Brown and Lil' Wayne. Talib looks at the phone and silences it.)

TALIB
Uh, Craig, it's getting late and I've got to get to a study group
anyway. Thanks for meeting with me, but I need to head out…

CRAIG
Talib, wait, wait, we still need to talk about declaring a major?

TALIB
It's OK, I'll stop back by and see you soon. I hadn't
REALLY made up my mind on a major yet anyway.

(TALIB stands up and to begin to leave).

I actually just wanted to stop by and meet you.

CRAIG
OK, but just tell me a lil' more about your
"pretending" right quick before you go?

TALIB
Aw, come on, man. You know the game better
than anybody. I GOT' TA go!

CRAIG
OK, but Talib...

TALIB
Man, call me "T".

CRAIG
(smiling)
OK, T, but if you need me...or if anything else happens,
CALL ME. Here's my card and cell number.

TALIB
(Looking at the card and smiling)
Hey, thanks. They said you was cool like that.

CRAIG
(Laughing)
Well, you know. I try.

(Both men give each other a fist bump and Talib
departs. Phone rings. CRAIG answers.)

CRAIG
Yes, Dean Roberts. Yes, yes, I met with him…He's a
good kid. A bit jumpy and stressed out…

(Dean comments in garbled shouting)

Wait, Dean, before you get worked up, you know how students are at
the beginning of the semester: excited, anxious, overwhelmed all rolled
into one… But he seems like a great student…major…no, we didn't
quite get to that…we were just checking in on a number of issues.

(Dean comments in garbled shouting)

CRAIG
…Just general talk about his summer, classes so far, stuff like that, nothing
major. Anyway, he's coming by again for a follow-up to get that done…

CRAIG
(curious)
Wait, why are so concerned about THIS STUDENT? I'm just
reviewing my roster of student advisees. By the way, why do
he and Alia Maqmood have asterisks by their names?

(Craig listening and frowning)

CRAIG
Discussions across the institution???… More scrutiny of
students on campus, huh?…We need to monitor CERTAIN

communities more closely--- (frowning)…uh-huh, uh-huh, uh,---yeah, I think I know exactly what you mean.

(CRAIG slams the phone down and rubs his chin pondering things).

CRAIG
Dammit. It's that kind of constant surveillance that…

(End of scene).

SCENE II

(Knock on the door of Craig's office. Angel, a Latina colleague from the Law School is standing in his door wearing an Islamic scarf and a sweat suit/running suit.)

ANGEL
Hey Craig. You ready?

CRAIG
Hey girl. Hey, come on in.

ANGEL
You know we got group in 30 minutes. What's wit' all this paperwork? Oh, I know., I know YOU and YOUR students as usual.

CRAIG
I'm just finishing up paperwork. The administration is a little nervous over a few students.

ANGEL
Academic concerns?

CRAIG
No...uh...just general concerns about certain students' adjustments to campus.

ANGEL
(Waving her finger)
CERTAIN students, huh? Yeah, ok, see, don't EVEN get started this shit, Craig?!

CRAIG
OK, OK, so let me ask you: Angel, you are a Cuban-American Muslim. How the fuck do you sort this shit out, I mean your loyalties and allegiances?

ANGEL

Listen, the shit is complicated. I AM AN AMERICAN, but I do
have family that live near Guantanamo in Cuba who are concerned
about what is happening there. And yes, I'm in law school to
help Muslims get due process AND to PROSECUTE stupid-ass
Muslims who engage in acts of terror against MY country---the
US of A. So, yeah, it's complicated, but hell, life is complicated.

(Craig laughs.)

CRAIG

Yeah, it's complicated…and you got a filthy-ass mouth.

ANGEL

Fuck you, Craig.

(Both laugh.)

CRAIG

Listen, I'm just concerned about this kid. He's bright, talented. Could
do anything. But might just be pissed off enough to be used…

ANGEL

Used? How? By who? Who is he? Tell me, I might know him.

CRAIG

I'd rather not get into specifics. When I say "used" I mean used
by folks looking for a kid FOR SOME GREAT CAUSE.

ANGEL

Craig, first watch your stereotypes. More importantly, though,
don't get tangled up in this too deep, just stay focused on your
work. You know your undergrad students are flaky and emotional,
living from moment to moment. They'll all be fine.

CRAIG
Yeah, but they still need OUR support. If we don't listen
and try to walk with these students, who will?

(End of Scene.)

SCENE III

(Actor sits on stage in the dark in the Muslim prayer position kneeling. The call to prayer is performed and the person repeats prostrations of Muslim prayer and then sits to listen to the imam (the prayer leader) of the mosque. Imam should be a mature individual with a faint accent.)

IMAM HAKIM

Welcome to new students and welcome back to others returning this semester. We here at Masjid al-Haqq greet you in the greeting words of peace of Assalamu Alaikum.

(Response from crowd in unison: Wa' Alaikum Salaam Wa Rahmutullah Wa Barakatuhu.)

IMAM HAKIM

In'shallah, you all had summer filled with opportunities to grow in your studies, but also spent time with family and friends before returning to campus. Yet, like too many school years in recent times, we return to campus with the continued challenges of being Muslim in America.

(INSERT CLIPS OF THE FOLLOWING LOCATIONS FROM THE EVENING NEWS)

IMAM HAKIM

Strikes in Iran, terrorist attacks in Pakistan, piracy in Somalia, continued wars in Iraq and Afghanistan, threats of attacks from Yemen. All of these things continue to test us, challenging us to stay true to our faith. International crises tend to "come right home to roost" on our doorsteps as Brother Malcolm X said many years ago.

(Actor continues to pray in the shadows.)

IMAM HAKIM

Our very bodies bear the mark of Islam: prayer beads around our wrists, scarves and skullcaps covering our heads, the brown marks on our foreheads from years of prostrating in prayer. YET, the choice to practice this faith comes with consequences. You might be followed. You might be questioned, stopped on campus, isolated in your classes, challenges by classmates. But you MUST maintain your dignity because we know that hard times purify...true "jihad" is not about holy war, but about striving to withstand the daily challenges of your lives while staying true to our faith.

Be clear, Beloved, I do not mean to alarm you---especially our new brothers and sisters. However, as your spiritual leader---a leader who is entrusted with your care while many of you are far from families---I just want you to be warned, alert and prepared concerning the storm clouds that might be on the horizon.

(The seated figure stands does one prostration of Islamic prayer and leaves the stage.)

(Talib is at the residence hall when Hanna, a perky white blond knocks on his door wearing a scarf, blousy top and jeans.) Talib is in bed reading VIBE magazine fiddling with his prayer beads. He rises to get the door).

TALIB

Hey Hanna, come on in, but leave the door open.

HANNA

(Returning greeting with great vigor)

Assalamu Alaikum!!!

TALIB

(Sighing heavily)

Wa'alaikum Salaam, Hanna. Girl, why you all geeked up? Just sit down.

HANNA

Come on, I need to practice my Arabic as often as possible. Kafl Hallish?

TALIB

(Rolling his eyes)

Bikayr Al-Hamdulilah. So, what you do you want? I'm trying to study, my roommate will be back soon and you KNOW he doesn't really like having you here.

HANNA

Why doesn't he want ME here?

TALIB

It's not personal, but he just doesn't like having women come to our room---especially women who we aren't dating, engaged to or married to.

HANNA

(Wailing)

But I'm your sister in ISLAM!

TALIB
(Getting annoyed)
Just respect his position--- even if you don't agree with it.
Anyway, Hanna, what do you need? I gotta study!

HANNA
Study? What class you takin' laying up here
reading about Drake and Weezy?

TALIB
Why you all up in my business? And why you
got all that shit on your hands?

HANNA
(Delighting in her hand designs):
I went to a henna party sponsored by the Muslim
Women's Association and got my hands decorated.

TALIB
I guess you ain't goin' home this weekend (He laughs). Your parents
would trip the fuck out when they see that shit on your hands.

HANNA
(Defiant)
They don't control me! I am a Muslim and proud
of it and I'll do what I want to do.

TALIB
Alright, Sister Souljah. Calm down!

HANNA
Oh, yeah, don't forget, Talib: Applications for the summer
language program in Yemen are due to Global Studies Program
by Friday. So, I wanted to bring you another flyer about it

(Hanna lays her purse on Bilal's desk and pulls out the papers)

I came by to see if you have your personal essay together. Remember,
didn't you mention that you might go on the Arabic program?

TALIB

Yemen? Hell, no. Are you fuckin' crazy? I get over there
and I'll never get my ass back in the country.

HANNA

(Fantasizing)

But it will be a chance to travel, live and study in the heart of Islam!

TALIB

Girl, I got enough problems, but you go head on 'cuz once you wash that
shit off your hands, you are still a white girl…and you'll be all right.

HANNA

How can you say things like that to me? You sound like
those racist kids at the Black Student Union meeting.

TALIB

Racist…why are THEY racist?

HANNA

Because they judge me too and make assumptions about my life
experiences. Why doesn't anyone understand. My life ISN'T perfect.

TALIB

(Regretful)

Listen, I'm sorry. It's just that we live in two different worlds in a
lot of ways. You are a new convert, I was born and raised Muslim
my whole life. You are female, I am male. You are white, I am South
Asian. So we are different, but that is no reason for me to discourage
you. (Sarcastically) Welcome to the faith and enjoy your journey.

HANNA
(Sighs)
Don't you enjoy it?

TALIB
No…I mean, sure I love Islam…but well, no, not all the
time…sigh…Listen, I love my faith, but it's complicated.
I am just trying to sort out where I stand.

HANNA
On what exactly?
(TALIB's phone goes off with a Gucci-Man ringtone.)

TALIB
(On the phone)
Yeah, yeah. Ah-right. Man, come on through. (To Hanna)
OK, that was Bilal. And I'm not dealing with another
fight between you two…so I NEED you to go.

HANNA
Why do you hang out with him when YOU
KNOW he doesn't like white people?

TALIB
See, that's what I mean. That's not even true, but see you're white one
minute and Muslim the next. (Exasperated) You don't have A CLUE.

HANNA
(Seething)
Why can't I be both???

(Hanna walks out of Talib's room and heads down the hallway
and bumps into Marty and Chris---two white guys who
were her former fraternity brothers on campus. Chris lives
on the floor, but Marty lives at the fraternity house.)

MARTY

Hey Hanna? What'chu doin' on our floor?

HANNA

(Hanna pulling on her scarf trying to avoid him)

Hey Marty. What's going on?

MARTY

Slow down, slow down. What's the rush? And why are
you wearing that scarf. You cold? Your hair wet?

HANNA

No, Marty, I actually...

MARTY

(Laughing and moving in close to Hanna)

Anyway, Hanna. Don't forget" we're having our annual "Crossing the
Border" party this weekend. You know, that's where we all dress up like
Mexicans, drink Tequila, get fuuuuuuuuuuuuuucked upppppppppp.

(Marty laughs)

CHRIS

(Embarassed)

Marty, I told you we decided to call it "International Night" INSTEAD.

MARTY

Ah, shit, I like the original name better. It just rings so true. You
don't know whose American and who is not these days. Even the
"President" won't even show us his REAL got-damn birth certificate?!

CHRIS

Marty, man, come on, cut that shit out.

HANNA

(Pressing the elevator door)

Sorry, Marty, I won't be there. I'm not really active in the sorority anymore.

CHRIS
Hey, Hanna, is it true?

HANNA
Is what true?

CHRIS
Well, I heard that you are "Muslamic" now? You know, down with Islam?

MARTY
Shut the fuck up, Chris. Ain't no way our girl Hanna is down with
"the Muslamics"…Not the way she used to drain a beer bong dry?

(Marty dances up to her as she backs away)

You know what we used to say, "Hanna, Hanna could choke
the shit out'cho banana…Hanna Hanna could suck the…

(The elevator door opens, Hanna---horrified---hops on
and escapes their taunts. Marty howls with delight.)

CHRIS
Marty, man, you are a REAL asshole.

(Just then, Bilal steps off the other elevator staring at Marty and
Chris. His arms are filled with books. Marty, recovering from
laughter is silent. Bilal is wearing a kufi---an Islamic prayer cap on
his head---a running jacket, jeans and Timberlands loosely tied.)

CHRIS
Wassup, B?

BILAL
(Hesitant)
'Sup, Chris?

(Bilal looks at Marty who says nothing.)

BILAL
See yall, later.

(Bilal rushes into his room with a stack of books
and throws them on the desk.)

BILAL
Salaama-Laikum, Bruh. How'se your day going?

TALIB
Wa-alaikum-salam, Bruh. I'm just chillin. How bout'chu?

BILAL
Man, you know how I do: I keep it busy. Gym early this morning.
Prayer. Grabbed breakfast. Two classes this morning. Prayer. Lunch.
Two labs this afternoon. Came home to chill a minute before prayer,
grab dinner and then gotta hit the library to study tonight. Got a
HUUUUUGE exam coming up and MCAT prep and then prayer.

TALIB
Bruh, you NEVER quit. You got to slow down sometime. Relax a little.

BILAL
That's easy for you to say. You are set financially.
Me, I got to keep grindin' ery' day.

TALIB
Whatchu' mean "SET"?

(Bilal looks over and notices a purse sitting on his desk and explodes).

BILAL
Dammit, T, SHE'S been up in here AGAIN?

23

TALIB
(Sheepishly)
WHO?

BILAL
(Grabbing the purse and shaking it)
HANNA. Hanna's been here again…and she left her purse?!

TALIB
Bilal, Bilal, bruh, calm down. She just stopped up here for a minute to
drop off some papers about the summer study abroad trip to Yemen.

BILAL
All it takes is a minute for folks to get the wrong idea.

TALIB
Why are you so worked up about this? We kept
the door open and everything?!

BILAL
'Cuz BOTH OF YALL are clueless. She's clueless about Islamic
etiquette and you are clueless about African-American history.
Don't we catch enough hell on this campus without more drama?

TALIB
Yeah. Ok, But we weren't…

BILAL
(Begging)
…SO WHYYYYYY you want to complicate our lives
by running around wit' some White girl?

TALIB
B, come on. First, I DO KNOW African American History, thank
you very much. Secondly, I ain't running around with her. But
thirdly, show her SOME respect. She is our sister in Islam.

BILAL

(Rolling his eyes)

SHE ain't none of my sister--- floating around here all non-
challant... without a clue as to what she's doing. YOU need to
be careful with her is all I'm saying. Give her some time to learn
more about the religion and get her mind right. Like I said,
you ain't got no worries, MR. MODEL MINORITY, but I got
to work twice as hard to get half as far, best believe that.

TALIB

B, I hear you, but you're trippin'. She's HARMLESS.

BILAL

Yeah, and that's what Emmett Till thought.

TALIB

EMMETT TILL?! THAT was a trillion years ago.

BILAL

So why do WE keep getting hate mail, getting our tires slashed, getting
stared at EVERY TIME we go to the showers ...or the cafeteria...
and getting stopped by campus police? Keep on, give 'em one more
excuse to fuck wit' us by messing with one of THEIR women?

TALIB

THEIR WOMEN? You know you sound like your granddaddy talking
like that? We get fucked wit' because of our religion, not our race.

(BILAL)

Oh, and you think they are bothering to separate the two. Listen, you
tell your story, I'll tell mine. Just because I am Muslim doesn't mean
I can forget my history---my African American history. And I know
you immigrant brothers WANT to be exceptional, but American
racism don't work that way, player---not even for you. Nobody ever
wants to be compared to African Americans--- but that's OK.

(Pointing his finger at Talib)
You gon' learn.

TALIB

B, man, you so full-a shit sometimes. Somedays I wonder
why the fuck I picked you for a roommate.

BILAL

...'Cuz you know I'm telling yo' ass the truth up in this piece. You
THINK you know BLACK FOLK, but the bruthas that worked
security out in front of your daddy's Seven-Elevens didn't count,
bruh. They couldn't tell you the truth 'cuz they worked for you. I--
-on the other hand--- I ain't got to sugarcoat SHIT for you, T.

TALIB

B, I hate to break it to you, but:
(Shouting)
THIS IS THE 21ST CENTURY. WE HAVE A BLACK
PRESIDENT WHOSE DAD WAS A MUSLIM. So you
got to leave some of your hangups at the door.

BILAL

But you see, that's just it. Look at the kind of hate he gets ON A DAILY
BASIS. He's got a whole movement against him chanting: "Go back
to Africa, Monkey". And those same have shut the government down.
That YOUR 21ST CENTURY AMERICA, BRUH. The hate is crazy-
high for folks who are scared that they have lost control of "their
country"...lost control of the non-whites in THEIR AMERICA...
and they pass those fears right on to their kids...so they fight
like hell to "TAKE AMERICA BACK"and all that bullshit.

TALIB

But that's just the point. In the midst of all that, Hanna doesn't hate us.
She has embraced us and Islam. That takes a helluva-lot of courage.

BILAL
(Sarcastically)
US??? She likes YOU…and would indeed EMBRACE YOU if you let her.

TALIB
(Chuckling)
Fool, she's just trying to find her way.

BILAL
Well, just keep her the hell-up out of here. This
ain't the path to paradise, Bruh.

TALIB
Ooooo, you so nasty?!

BILAL
Astagfir-Allah! (God forgive me!) I'm just trying to stay alive! We are men
of color AND we are Muslim. So, if that white girl breaks a nail up-in-here
and leaves outta here crying or upset, we gon' catch hell. I PROMISE YOU
THAT. MAN, TAKE MY MU' FUCKIN' WORD…JUST TRUST ME.

TALIB
Bruh, you crazy.

BILAL
T, please, just trust me and do this for me. If you won't trust history,
just trust the fact that she's a new Muslim and needs to get grounded
in the faith for herself…without all of YOUR HELP, you here me?

TALIB
OK, OK, I hear you.

(End of Scene.)

(TALIB is outside of an office door knocking. On the other side of the desk is a woman seated at a desk reading a stack of papers.)

TALIB

Dr. Evers, you wanted to see me?

DR. EVERS

Yes, yes, Talib come in.

(TALIB eases in to the office slowly, uneasily, removing his hat.)

DR. EVERS

(Smiling)

Talib, you know you are one of the few students that still remove their hats?! It's a sign of manners and great parenting.

TALIB

Yeah, well my mother doesn't tolerate it, so I figure professors won't either.

DR. EVERS

Well, Talib. I asked to come by because I wanted to talk with you about your course essay.

TALIB

(Swallowing hard.)

OK, sure.

DR. EVERS

Now, don't get me wrong. Your essay was very well written and well argued. There was just one passage I wanted to discuss. Talib, your paper is about student activism on college campuses during the 1960s. You provide a thorough overview of how students clashed with local police and military on campus over the war in Vietnam. However, I wanted to talk to you about this passage. Can you read the part I highlighted?

TALIB
(TALIB holding on to his essay)

"In reflecting on the student activism of this era, it is amazing to consider how difficult it was for students during that time on college campuses. I always imagined college campuses to be places where students were free to express themselves, and free to examine other faiths, practices, institutions belief systems---even the ones they disagreed with. Yet, fifty years later, students on campuses are STILL stigmatized, judged, mistreated.

DR. EVERS
(Shaking her head with a furled brow):
OK, you can stop right there. You mention
"faith". What do you mean by it?

TALIB
(Sighs)
You know, Dr. Evers, "faith", "religion", "one's religious practice".

DR. EVERS
(Nervous)
Can you say more about this?

TALIB
(Sighs)
I was just saying that campuses are not safe places for students whose race, class, faith or sexuality differ from the "norms" of campus. And on this campus, the "norms" are white, Greek, suburban, focused on athletics, getting drunk and having sex as often as possible.

DR. EVERS
(Becoming defensive)
First of all, Talib, THIS campus IS a diverse spaces with students from all kinds of backgrounds and persuasions.

TALIB

OK, Dr. Evers, but I'm not talking about the school's brochure
propaganda, I'm talking about THE REAL DEAL, here, on the ground.

DR. EVERS
(Exasperated)

But, come on, Talib. Is this really YOUR experience? You are an Asian
student after all and----if you don't mind me saying---Asian students
are represented in large numbers on campus and tend to do quite
well in higher education compared to other non-white students.

TALIB
(Tensing and sighing)
What do you mean?

DR. EVERS

Well, our Asian students---like yourself--- are focused, hardworking,
from good families, industrious, hardly ever complain about
life on campus and don't keep up "trouble" on campus. You
all don't do protests and YOU ALL fit in here very well.

TALIB

Well---if you don't mind me saying---all "ASIANS" are not the
same. And "my kind of Asian"---namely dark-skinned Muslim
South Asians---get a fair amount of grief on this campus.

(Sucking his teeth exasperated)

DR. EVERS
(Shocked)

Talib, I never knew you were going through so much. It
never comes out in class. You are always so calm.

TALIB

I GOTTA BE CALM. There's no room in the classroom for the Muslim
kid to get loud or say anything controversial. Folks are scared enough of
me as it is. So, I just share my ideas with you in my papers---not out loud.

DR. EVERS
You are a very strong writer and great student. Would you
feel comfortable discussing any of these issues in class?

TALIB
(TALIB jumps up)
Helllllllllll, no, Dr. E.!!! Ooops, excuse me, Dr. E. But, I don't
need any more attention. Besides, it's YOUR JOB TO RAISE
THE ISSUES YOU WANT TO DISCUSS, NOT ME. If
you want to do a retrospective of campus climate then and
now, feel free and I MIGHT wade into the discussion. But
PLEEEAAASSSEEEE don't call on me to bring anything up.

DR. EVERS
Talib, I stand corrected. You are indeed right. But, I want to know what I
can do to make you feel more safe on campus, more comfortable in class?

TALIB
Thank you for your concern, Dr.E, but the reality is that the only
secure space I have is the seat I sit in most days...and that's just
the way it is. But I'm good...REALLY. I just want to be in the
class like everyone else and able to share my ideas openly and
honestly IF AND WHEN I CHOSE TO. Anything else, Dr. E?

DR. EVERS
(Mystified by the conversation)
No...uh, no Talib. But thanks for coming by.

TALIB
OK, I'll see you Tuesday.

(TALIB shakes her hand, puts his hat back on and exits her office.)

(Hanna and Angel meet up after prayers to chat.
They sit on a bench together outdoors.)

HANNA

Sister Angel, thanks so much for being willing to meet with me.

ANGEL

Oh, it's no problem at all, HANNA. I'm glad to do it. It's always
great to get to know new sisters. It keeps all of us excited to see the
new Muslims grow in their faith---especially new American sisters.
And, you can just call me "Angel". We just use "sister" when we are
in the company of children as a term of respect; or when brothers
are addressing women they are not married to for respect as well.

HANNA

OK, Angel! IT's just nice to have sisters who you can talk to who are "real
", you know: in the world like I am, in school, working, etc.,. And I wanted
to talk with you because I am still STRUUUUU-GLING in one area.

ANGEL

(Laughing to herself)

Just ONE area? Lucky you! No really, Hanna. Go easy on yourself.
Converting is a HUGE LIFE CHANGE: dressing differently, fasting,
praying five times a day, offering a portion of your earnings to charity,
planning to make the pilgrimage to Hajj, changes in your friends,
family, how you socialize with folks---it's a lot to adust to in the
beginning for anybody. How is your family adjusting to all this?

HANNA

They have been pretty cool about it. I mean, we weren't very religious
to start with. So, I think they think that having some kind of faith life
is fine---even this one. But I think it's tough for them to get used to my
changes in diet, dress and the fact that I don't drink anymore. I was a
HUGE boozer so my dad can hardly believe it…and he's grateful for

that change most of all. They see that I'm more serious, done partying and dating crappy guys, spending more time on my studies and pray a lot…so they say "Hallelujah" for any religion that can do that.

ANGEL
(Laughing out loud)
OK, so, if it 's not family, what's the big challenge?

HANNA
(Hanging her head and blushing, hopping up and then howling)
IT'S MENNNNNN!!!!!
(Both women fall out laughing because she is so earnest AND loud)

ANGEL
Girl, YOU are A MESS!

HANNA
I KNOW, I KNOW I AM, ANGEL! But that's my problem…
(Whispering)
…My lust for men…See, back in the day before I was Muslim…

ANGEL
(Cutting her off)
…You mean YESTERDAY?!

HANNA
ANGELLLLLLLLL!!!

ANGEL
OK, OK, I'm sorry. Go 'head. Go 'head.

HANNA
Well, before I converted, I used to…

(Voice gets deep getting nostalgic and she dances
around doing some seductive dancing)

I USE TO KIIIIIICK IT, ANGEL. I would drink, dance---I
mean like crazy-stripper-pole dance-type stuff, Angel---and
HAAAANG OUT with the fellas. I think I just wanted the
attention. And with so many girls in sororities (or not) trying to
get attention, I'd do crazier and riskier stuff just to stand out.

ANGEL
(Sympathetic)
So, Hanna, if you were having ALL THAT FUN, why did you convert?

HANNA
(Sighing)
'Cuz that shit got OLD, Angel. I just got tired of waking up
sick and NOT KNOWING what I did…or WHO I had been
with…. or what the hell happened the night before.

ANGEL
OK, well, I can understand cooling some of
that out…but why CONVERT?

HANNA
Well, I did still go to classes. And there was this guy…

ANGEL
Astagfir-allah (God, forgive it), a guy???

HANNA
No, no, really, it wasn't like that. He was in Dr. Ever's Faith and
Society class. And he was really interesting to listen to. So when
he did his presentation on "Faith and Family", he talked about
growing up Muslim and how prayer and the Ramadhan fast and
the diversity of the community kept him connected to God…
THAT path, THAT tradition, THAT clarity just spoke to me.

ANGEL
(Standing and crossing her arms suspiciously)
And did he talk about the role of women in Islam?

HANNA
Actually, he did. He explained that women covered or dressed
modestly to keep the focus on their minds and abilities and not their
bodies. And he talked about how women were supposed to keep
their beauty to themselves and for their families and husbands.

(Angel nods affirmatively)

When I heard him say that, I just felt "relief". I said to myself: You mean,
I don't have to drink and clown and wear tight shit to matter in this
world?! Now, THAT'S cool. The idea that I could cover myself up and
function in the world was just a revelation to me. I had never gotten that
message from family or my peers or the media or anybody before.

ANGEL
Al-hamduliah. That brother sounds sweet and
clear in his understanding of Islam.

HANNA
(Blushing)
Oh, he is. HE IS.

ANGEL
(Being dramatic and swooning and crying to the heavens)
Now, she wouldn't be the first. But Allah (SWT), please
don't tell me she converted FOR A MAN???

HANNA
(Adamant)
NO, NO Angel. REALLY. ISLAM---not him---has made me think
more globally about history, culture, language, everything, than ever

before. THE RELIGION just opened my mind up, MY WORLD UP to travel, study, meeting people from all over the world.

ANGEL
…And???

HANNA
(Convincing herself)
Ok, Angel, Ok. YES, HE'S AMAZING, but WE'RE JUST FRIENDS. And besides, I really don't know how to manage things in that area anyway…as a Muslim and all.

ANGEL
…Things like what?

HANNA
…Like dating, going out, all that.

ANGEL
Hanna, take it slow. For now, I think if you just concentrate on your practice, your studies and socialize with men---Muslim or not---in public and in groups, you'll find you have plenty to work on right now.

HANNA
Yeah, Angel, you are probably right. It's just hard because this brother lives on the same floor as this guy I used to mess around with in the fraternity, but he was a clown so I dropped him like that (snap).

ANGEL
Wait, wait, WAIT! What are you doing going up to ANY male floors?

HANNA
Talib and I are in some of the same classes so some times---when I need help with class I'll go up and…

ANGEL

(Shaking her head in a definitive "no")

Uh-huh, Hanna. Ok, first, yeah, ok, Talib is a cutie. But---more to the point---you can talk to Talib in classes, cafes, libraries, PUBLIC SPACES, but you can't go up to his room or be with him in his room alone. It's just TOO TEMPTING. And the saying goes, if you two unmarried folk are alone, the Shaytan (The Devil) is ALWAYS present and whispering.

HANNA

(Wailing)

Uhhhhhhhhhhhh!!! Why does SO much have
to change now that I'm a Muslim!!!

ANGEL

The other piece is this: Hanna, aren't Talib and Bilal roommates?

HANNA

Yeah, why?

ANGEL

...Well as men of color who are also Muslim, it's just not
appropriate for you to be up there all the time.

HANNA

Ok, you explained their Islamic part about temptation,
but what does their color have to do with it?

ANGEL

Men of color have caught a lot of hell at times for being in the wrong place at the wrong time with White women. So, for their sakes, just stay clear of their room and hang out with them in public, ok?

HANNA

Angel, why do we have to give up so much as Muslims?

ANGEL

Hanna, Islam means "submission" or one who submits to the will of Allah (SWT). So we have to struggle to submit our ways to God's ways. We have to resist our will---and our flesh at times---to do what Allah requires of us.

(Hanna sighs heavily)

So, because you are a new Muslim, give yourself a chance to get strong by avoiding temptations. I'm telling you sister, it's for the best.

HANNA
(Mischevously)
Angel, do you have anyone special in your life?

ANGEL
(Blushing)
Girl, please, as busy as I am, I don't have time for....

(Hanna cuts her off)

HANNA
Angelllllllllllllll, tell me!

ANGEL
OK, OK, let's just say I'm just praying about a few things in that area right now...It's complicated. AND THAT'S THAT!

HANNA
(Giving up the probing questions)
Well, in'shallah, things will work out and we'll both get what we want.

ANGEL
(Taking Hanna's arm)
Come on. Let's go get something to eat. It'll be time to pray soon.

SCENE II

(Bilal is watching the President on television when Talib
comes into their room singing with his headphones on.)

BILAL

Shhh, shhh, hey man, hold all that down, the President is on.

TALIB

Why? What's wrong? Somethin' happen?

BILAL

Naw, man, you know tonight is his speech on his plan for Afghanistan.

TALIB

That's right, that's right. I forgot. TURN IT UP! TURN IT UP!

(The two young men sit transfixed as President speaks; intercut
footage audibly or on screen from the President.)

REMARKS BY THE PRESIDENT IN ADDRESS TO THE NATION
ON THE WAY FORWARD IN AFGHANISTAN AND PAKISTAN

EISENHOWER HALL THEATRE, UNITED STATES MILITARY
ACADEMY AT WEST POINT, WEST POINT, NEW YORK

8:01 P.M. EST

THE PRESIDENT: GOOD EVENING. TO THE UNITED
STATES CORPS OF CADETS, TO THE MEN AND
WOMEN OF OUR ARMED SERVICES, AND TO MY
FELLOW AMERICANS: I WANT TO SPEAK TO YOU
TONIGHT ABOUT OUR EFFORT IN AFGHANISTAN.
WE DID NOT ASK FOR THIS FIGHT. ON SEPTEMBER 11, 2001,
19 MEN HIJACKED FOUR AIRPLANES AND USED THEM TO
MURDER NEARLY 3,000 PEOPLE. THEY STRUCK AT OUR

MILITARY AND ECONOMIC NERVE CENTERS. THEY TOOK
THE LIVES OF INNOCENT MEN, WOMEN, AND CHILDREN
WITHOUT REGARD TO THEIR FAITH OR RACE OR STATION...

THEN, IN EARLY 2003, THE DECISION WAS MADE TO
WAGE A SECOND WAR, IN IRAQ. -- AND THAT THE
DECISION TO GO INTO IRAQ CAUSED SUBSTANTIAL RIFTS
BETWEEN AMERICA AND MUCH OF THE WORLD...

BUT WHILE WE'VE ACHIEVED HARD-EARNED
MILESTONES IN IRAQ, THE SITUATION IN
AFGHANISTAN HAS DETERIORATED.

AND AS COMMANDER-IN-CHIEF, I HAVE DETERMINED
THAT IT IS IN OUR VITAL NATIONAL INTEREST TO SEND
AN ADDITIONAL 30,000 U.S. TROOPS TO AFGHANISTAN...

(Both men begin to scream and yell obscenities at the television.)

TALIB
Ah, man, you can turn that shit off now.

(BILAL sits stone faced in silence.)

TALIB
Bilal, Bilal, man you all right?

BILAL
Nah man, I'm confused as hell. I voted for Obama because I wanted
his ass TO END THE WAR. Now, he's sending 30,000 MORE troops
INTO Afghanistan---another Muslim country. Shit, I got family in the
military and I don't want to see them die in another dumb-ass war.

TALIB
(Pacing)
I KNOW MAN, I KNOW. It's like he has to GO OUT OF HIS
WAY TO BE HARD ON MUSLIMS to overcompensate for
having Muslims in his family and growing up in Indonesia.

(BILAL stands up and throws down his pillow.)

BILAL
Ahhhhhhhhhhhhhh. THIS is so fuckin' disappointing.

TALIB
Well, at least he's saying it will be over in eighteen months.

BILAL
Aw, man, you can't believe that shit. He said the Health Care bill would
be done in August of 2009 and you see how long that shit took.

TALIB
(Laughing)
Yeah, OK, man, you do have a point there.

BILAL
Talib, man, sometimes, I really do think folks got it in for us
Muslims. But, I thought this Black President with Muslim
roots would be TIRED fighting wars against Muslims
THAT OUR NATION CAN'T EVEN AFFORD.

TALIB
It's like HE DOESN'T EVEN SEE US.
…And in countries where you have bombs being dropped
on you EVERYDAY and YOUR towns are destroyed, your
neighbors killed, you have no stability…you just want to fight
back and defend yourself BY ANY MEANS NECESSARY.

(Both men look at each other and fall out laughing.)

BILAL
(Getting serious)
No, man, but fa' real, what are you saying?

TALIB
All I'm saying is that Americans---including the President---
seem to be able to support wars that DON'T rain down on their
fuckin' heads night and day. And THAT SHIT is fucked up!

BILAL
So, what we gon' do?

TALIB
I'ma write 'em and our other elected officials and
let him know how I feel for starters.

BILAL
OK, let's get to written, bruh.

(Talib hops up and gets on his computer as Bilal stand
behind him. Later that night, Bilal takes a moment to
talk with his brother, Jonathan on the phone.)

BILAL
Hey, bruh, how you livin'?

JONATHAN
We're cool? Just got our orders from the Commander-In-Chief.

BILAL
I know, man, it's terrible.

JONATHAN
No man, it's fine. That's our job. We go where he sends us.

BILAL

Yeah, I'm just sick of them send us to the Muslim world.

JONATHAN

Whew, man I'll be glad when this "phase" is over.

BILAL

If by "phase" you mean "Islam", it's here to stay.

JONATHAN

So, how's your boy doin'? Has he asked you to
work at his dad's store this summer?

BILAL

Jon, man, why you trippin'? Talib's my boy. He's
good people. Hell, no, he hasn't.

JONATHAN

Are you sure about that?

BILAL

HE'S my brother.

JONATHAN

No, I'MMMM your brother. He's yo' roommate…
gotchu hidin' up under that skullcap.

BILAL

You mean like you hidin' in them Army fatigues??? Don't act
like yo' war is so righteous, bruh. You better watch yo' back.

JONATHAN

Is that a threat?

BILAL

No bruh., I'm just lettin' you know that some folk don't
appreciate unjust wars that's all I'm sayin'.

JONATHAN

We done? I think we need to be done with this conversation.

BILAL

Hey, bruh. It's on you. I'm done.

JONATHAN

Listen, man. We not on opposite sides of this. You are my brother
and I know Talib is a good guy. I'm just messin' with'chu.

BILAL

I know. I know. I just hate that you have to war against Muslims.

JONATHAN

B, I LOVE YOU.

BILAL

You know I got this, man. I love you MORE.
(Both men hang up.)

(Footage on the Fort Hood Massacre chaos after the shooting is shown to audience. CRAIG enters the stage to take his seat at a desk. Lights come up and BILAL---Talib's roommate--- is on the phone, frantic with Fort Hood news coverage playing in the background.)

BILAL
...Mama, mama, come on now, I know Jon is at Fort Hood, but Jonathan is smart and tough and well-trained. Ma, ma, I'm sure he took cover and is somewhere helping other folks. OK, OK, go head, get the other line and I'll call you if I hear anything.

(Bilal slams the phone down.)

TALIB
Man, I'm so sorry to hear about your brother. Can I do anything?

BILAL
(Pacing and distracted)
Aw, man. Jon'll be fine. I just wish he'd call. Moms is worried sick. How the fuck could OUR brother do this... how could A FELLOW MUSLIM do this to fellow soldiers???

TALIB
Man, clearly, he was fucked up in the head and just snapped. The pressure to be a soldier combined with the pressure to be a Muslim in the military was just too much for 'em and he...

BILAL
So, he just kills a bunch of Americans???

TALIB
Bruh, the shooter is AN AMERICAN, too! Look, look, I'm not making excuses for 'em. THIS SHIT HERE IS TERRIBLE. I'm just tryin' to make some sense of it my damn self.

BILAL

You know, when I converted to Islam, I thought I chose a
better path..."you know, one God, universal truths, global
vision, diverse community"...all that shit. Now, I'm not so
sure...It's just one fuckin' headache after another.

(Knock at the door. Bilal and Talib look at each other.)

TALIB

I'm not expecting anybody?

(Talib hops up to get the door. It's Hanna on the other side. She is wearing
a white scarf with a few blond strands showing and long white garment.)

HANNA

(Sauntering in)

Assalamu Alaikum, brothers.

(Hanna saunters into the room as Bilal looks at her and
turns away rolling his eyes and sucking his teeth.)

TALIB

(TALIB still at the door watching her move around the room.)

Uh, Hanna...We were kinda' in the middle of something...

HANNA

(Oblivious)

You all notice anything different about me?

BILAL

(Seething)

Nope, you're the same ole pushy, bullshit dame you've always been.

HANNA

(Turning violently)

Bilal, you shut your mouth. How can you talk to me like that? Especially
when I'm wearing hijab AND jilbab. I'm your SISTER in Islam??

BILAL

(Getting in her face)

Girl, please. You're nuts. A crazy-ass Muslim JUUUUSSSTTTT
killed a gang of American soldiers and you pick TODAY---
this fuckin' day---to start wearin' Muslim overgarments...
you are INDEED trouble. All day long.

HANNA

(Angry and undeterred)

I am a PROUD MUSLIM WOMAN and now is the
time for me to show my support for our faith.

BILAL

Yeah, well if you so gotdamn proud, push that blond as hair up
under that scarf and be a Muslim woman FOR REAL.

HANNA

What does my hair have to do with anything?

BILAL

(Furious now)

The point of wearing hijab is to cover your hair COMPLETELY so
as not to draw attention to your hair, your body in general. But also,
in a society where hair color & texture, complexion and skin color
STILL MATTER, exposing your hair let's people know that you are
a White woman and allows you to still benefit from that privilege.

(Sigh).

The rest of us who don't have blond hair or light skin or blue eyes
catch it harder than you EVERY DAY OF EVERY WEEK.

(Looking at Talib)

Don't you get tired of explaining shit to her? Fuck
it, man, I'm done. She's YOUR project.
(Pushing past Hanna)

I'm up. Text me when she's gone.

(Bilal pushes past her and leaves.)

HANNA
(Shaken and angered)
HE'S an asshole. Why do you put up with him?

TALIB
(Defensive)
His brother was stationed at Fort Hood and he's missing...
and his mom is hella-worried right now.

HANNA
(Shocked, embarassed by her own behavior)
Ohhhh....man, I'm sorry to hear that.

TALIB
(Infuriated)
That's why I was trying to tell you we were in the middle of somethin',
but your "fashion show" was more important than what we were doing.

HANNA
(Regretful at first, then defensive)
I'm sorry about his brother ...and all but that
doesn't give him a right to be nasty to me!

TALIB
Hanna, you are right, absolutely right, but it's complicated. You still benefit
from being White....Just look at how folk fall all over you at the mosque?

"Oh, sister, your skin is so pretty. Ohhhhhhhh, sister, do your eyes always change colors, green one day, blue the next. Ohhhhhhhh, sister, are your married? You should meet my brother." Meanwhile, the brown-skinned sisters get no play. We Muslims are as color-conscious as anybody.

(Hanna hangs her head)

I'm Pakistani, but depending on the day, I'm either the model minority or terrorist #1. Meanwhile, Bilal is constantly harassed, followed, asked for ID by campus police just to be on campus because he's a Black man---even though he's a fuckin' pre-med student with a 3.94/4.0 GPA.

(Hanna plops on the bed)

HANNA
Damn, I thought converting to Islam would be an opportunity
to live in an easier, more diverse, spiritual, race neutral
space, but it's not. It's just one headache after another.

TALIB
(smirking)
Would you believe Bilal JUST said the same thing?

(HANNA and TALIB look at each other for a long time.)

TALIB
Hanna, why are you here?

HANNA
Because I wanted YOU TO SEE ME in my new hijab and jilbab.

TALIB
(Wincing)
You gon' wear that all the time...like from now on?

HANNA

Absolutely, like I said, to represent my faith PROUDLY.

TALIB

But you know you don't HAVE TO do all that. Especially
now. You don't have to PROVE your faith to anybody.

HANNA

But I want to…

TALIB

Listen, I don't have anything against this. But things are so crazy right
now. I don't need another thing to worry about…and I don't want you
to get jumped or hurt or worse because of how you are dressed.

HANNA

(Coyly)

It that all…or is there something else?

TALIB

Like what?

HANNA

Like are you worried about being in a relationship with me?

TALIB

(Furious)

RELATIONSHIP??? Oh, hell no. We ain't in no
relationship. Hanna, you are a nice girl and all, but…

HANNA

(Upset)

Oh, so I would have had a better shot with you if I had come up in here
in a hoe-fit (whore's outfit) like one of the trashy girls on campus.

TALIB

What? Nobody, said that.

HANNA

Yeah, you Muslim guys are all alike. You lead women to
the faith, but then when it's time to commit...

TALIB

Wait, wait, lead women to the faith? LEAD A WOMAN TO
THE FAITH? COMMIT? I didn't lead you nowhere. I thought
Allah (SWT) led you to this faith. We have classes together and
started talking. But if you notice, I don't come by your room
seeking you out for shit. So don't start with me about me being
a flaky Muslim guy; that ain't me. I'm not THAT GUY.

HANNA

(Sniffling)

And you had no idea I was interested in you?

TALIB

Dammit, Hanna, sometimes, YOU ARE just like most white
girls who think all they have to do is let down their hair, bat their
eyes and have men chasing them. Well, that ain't me either.

HANNA

(Insistent)

Talib, I really like you.

TALIB

And that's all that matters right, Hanna. You've never given me any room
or time to figure out if I like you at all. I just need a fucking break from...

HANNA

From what? From me?

TALIB
(Enraged)
From EVERY-FUCKIN' THING. School. Being
Muslim. Campus. Classes. Racism. Everything.

HANNA
(Rising to go, then hesitating)
OK, well, I give you some space…but can I text you later?

(Talib just glares at her, roars with laughter
and throws a pillow at the door.)

HANNA
(Unbowed)

OK, not tonight, not tonight, but I'll hit you up soon.

(Laughing)

OK, I'm gone.

(Talib falls back on the bed and the phone rings. Yet, he doesn't
move even when he hears Craig's voice on the machine.)

CRAIG
Hello! Hello?

(Message on the phone plays and is audible to audience.)

"Wassup, this is Talib and Bilal's spot. Leave a message and we'll
get back to you as soon as possible, ya here. Salaamu Alaikum.)

(Both men are clowning and laughing before the beep.)

CRAIG

Hello? Talib. Talib, this is Craig Davis, you advisor. (Anxious) I am calling to follow up on our meeting. We need to get your major declared so you need to stop by and see me so we can talk…

OK…and fa' real with all this Fort Hood mess goin' on, man, I, I, just wanted to check in on you and make sure you all are being careful. So, hit me up, man. Hit me up when you get this message, email me or at least text me to let me know that you are OK and when we can meet.

(Hanna races down the hallway and bumps into Marty who is in shock and tipsy when he see's her in her jilbab.)

MARTY
Hanna?

HANNA
(Hanna keeps walking)

MARTY
HAAAAAAAANAH!

HANNA
WHHHHHAAAAAATTTTTTT Marty?

MARTY
I heard you had become "Muslamic", but this "get up" is too much?!

HANNA
Marty, move, I GOTTA GO.

MARTY
(Holding her arm as Hanna pushing her scarf away)

Hanna, what the hell happened TO YOU???
(Caressing her face)
You were the nice, sweet, sorority girl…now, you're a TERRORIST.

HANNA
(Shouting, strong and serious)
Marty, get the hell out of my way RIGHT NOW.
(Marty relents and Hanna disappears.)

SCENE IV

LIGHTS GO DOWN; INTERCUT FOOTAGE
FROM THE PRESIDENT.

REMARKS BY THE PRESIDENT AT
MEMORIAL SERVICE AT FORT HOOD

FORT HOOD - III CORPS, FORT HOOD, TEXAS

1:55 P.M. CST

THE PRESIDENT: TO THE FORT HOOD COMMUNITY;
TO ADMIRAL MULLEN; GENERAL CASEY; GENERAL
CONE; SECRETARY MCHUGH; SECRETARY GATES; MOST
IMPORTANTLY, TO FAMILY, FRIENDS AND MEMBERS
OF OUR ARMED FORCES. WE COME TOGETHER FILLED
WITH SORROW FOR THE 13 AMERICANS THAT WE
HAVE LOST; WITH GRATITUDE FOR THE LIVES THAT
THEY LED; AND WITH A DETERMINATION TO HONOR
THEM THROUGH THE WORK WE CARRY ON....

IT MAY BE HARD TO COMPREHEND THE TWISTED
LOGIC THAT LED TO THIS TRAGEDY. BUT THIS
MUCH WE DO KNOW -- NO FAITH JUSTIFIES THESE
MURDEROUS AND CRAVEN ACTS; NO JUST AND LOVING
GOD LOOKS UPON THEM WITH FAVOR. FOR WHAT HE
HAS DONE, WE KNOW THAT THE KILLER WILL BE MET
WITH JUSTICE -- IN THIS WORLD, AND THE NEXT.

(Fade to black.)

(Lights come up again as Talib and Hanna are coming from
a study group at the library. Talib is racing ahead of her
impatiently. Hanna's scarf keeps slipping off her head.)

TALIB
Come on, girl. Hurry up. It's cold out and I don't
like being out late at night these days.

HANNA
I'm sorry, I didn't mean to leave my purse under
the table. Besides, what's the hurry?

(HANNA Grabbing his arm to slow him down.)

It's a beautiful night.

TALIB
(TALIB pulling away from her)
The only reason I'm out here with you is because
we were both headed back to the hall.

(Out of nowhere, several students emerge and
surround TALIB and HANNA.)

STUDENT
Would you look at this shit? A sand-niggas with one of OUR women.

TALIB
Come on man, I'm just walking her home. She ain't my girl.

STUDENT
Listen to him talking, yall. Talking like a nigga and
looking like Osama. You got double the trouble.

HANNA
(Anxious)
Come on, guys, were JUST friends.

(Hanna tries to press pass the guys.)

STUDENT #3
(Pushing Hanna back viciously)
Shut up, you Osama-lovin' bitch. We'll show you
how-to-fuck a terrorist.

IMAM HAKIM
Assalamu Alaikum Wa Rahmutullah Wa Barakatuhu! I greet you all,
my brothers and sisters, in the greeting words of peace of our faith.

(Congregants offer a lackluster "Wa Alaikum Salaam" in
unison from the congregants in a heavy serious tone.)

IMAM HAKIM
From your response, I sense the heaviness in your voices that must
have something to do with the recent events at Fort Hood and the
wave of anti-Muslim violence that has followed. I am sure you all
are filled with a mix of emotions---sadness for the victims, outrage
at the accused, fear of reprisals against Muslims across this country
and yet---if we are honest perhaps somewhere---some of us might
also be asking the question: How can the US continue to war
against Muslim countries and think there won't be backlash?

(Groans of agreement from the crowd)

But, brothers and sisters, he was an enlisted serviceman and had to
have known that--- in these times when the US has been at war against
Muslim countries for a decade--- he might be called to fight against
some Muslim country. So, he was wrong to enlist if he knew he had such
anti-war feelings and could not serve his country or fellow officers.

But the broader issue is this: we must reflect deeply on our own identities and loyalties. Are you a Muslim first or an American first?

Now regardless of your answer, I issue a challenge to you. This question is one that many other communities of color struggle with that many of our Caucasian brothers and sisters don't understand.

My question to you is this: Can you choose peace in this time or war? If you identify as Muslim, can we unite with other Muslims IN THE CAUSE OF PEACE? If you identify as an American, can you work with Americans of all faiths TO PROMOTE THE CAUSE OF PEACE?

(More groans from crowd.)

I know it is very VERY difficult to even think about peace when you feel under siege, attacked, profiled. However, if you say Islam is the faith of peace, when will we as Muslims step up and end the violence against the innocent---even as violence is being inflicted fellow Muslims?

(End of scene.)

---Intermission—

(Scene opens with Craig meeting Angel at the hospital.)

CRAIG
Hey Angel.
(They hug one another.)

Thanks for the text. WHAT in the hell happened?

ANGEL
(Speaking in hushed tones and moving him away from Hanna)
Talib's been admitt ed with broken ribs, cuts, facial lacerations.

(Craig fighting to hide the tears.)

CRAIG
Can I see him?

ANGEL
He's resting. But, they will both need counseling. Dr.
Aziz will let us know when he can have visitors.

CRAIG
Both? Who else was there?

ANGEL
Oh, sorry, the young woman---Hanna--- sitting over there is a
friend of his. She was with him when the attack happened. She's
also a new sister in Islam. She just converted a few months ago.

(Craig walks over to Hanna.)

CRAIG
Hi, Hanna. I'm Craig Davis, Talib's advisor...

HANNA
(Sniffling, standing up, scarf slipping backwards as usual)
Hi Mr. Davis. I've heard Talib talk about you before. He really likes you...

(Hanna breaks down and falls against Craig sobbing)

...I don't understand, Mr. Davis, why would they did this...

(ANGEL holds her--- trying to comfort her patting her back
and shaking her head at CRAIG. The lights go down.)

SCENE II

(The lights come up. BILAL sits in a chair on stage at the bedside of TALIB watching TALIB sleeping and reflecting. TALIB begins to stir in the bed writhing in pain. His face is covered with bruises. BILAL rises quietly to check on TALIB)

BILAL

Hey, hey, T, how you feelin'? You need anything?

(Talib carefully rolls over in the bed away from BILAL.)

TALIB

(Moaning loudly)

Uhhhhhhhhhhhhhh, I feel like shiiiiiiittttt!

BILAL

(Anxious)

Do you need a nurse for anything?

TALIB

(With labored breathing)

Nah, I just need to find a spot on this bed that doesn't hurt. WHAT are you doing here. I thought you were going to Texas with your Moms to get Jonathan's things.

BILAL

Mr. Davis contacted me and I had to come.
Actually, Mama insisted that I come.

TALIB

(Shaking his head and getting emotional)

Man, your Moms is something else!!! Her son get's killed by some crazy Muslim and she sends you here to be with me??? SHE'S REALLY AMAZING!!!

BILAL
(Choked up as well and clearing his throat)
...Well she sends you her best. You know Mama believes that two wrongs never make a right...they just make two damn wrongs!!!

BILAL
(Feeling horribly)
Talib, man, I'm soooooooooooooo sorry that this happened to you. But Mr. Davis said that Hanna went in and gave a description of the guys to campus security and the local police are working on the case.

(TALIB breaks into laughing painfully, coughing at times.)

TALIB
The police??? Campus security??? Are you fucking kidding me??

(Talib starts coughing.)

You think they gon' work hard IN THIS TOWN to find some White boys who beat the shit out of a "sand-nigger"???!!! Man, you can forget that.

(BILAL sighs.)

TALIB
Oohh, man, I'm sorry for using the "N" word.

BILAL
That's OK, man. I know what you are saying.

(TALIB rolls over and begins to sob quietly. BILAL walks over and touches his back. TALIB jumps.)

TALIB
(Pounding the bed)
It wasn't right. It wasn't right.

(Sobbing)

My dumb ass had to try to be damn gentleman and wait on Hanna's ass.
(Pounding the bed).

BILAL
(Emotional, but grabbing his arm to stop him from pounding the bed)

Listen to me. You didn't do anything wrong and neither
did Hanna. THIS WAS NOT YOUR FAULT. You all were
attacked--- so don't you blame yourself on her for this.

(TALIB with his back to Bilal, mumbling, but concerned...)

TALIB
Was she hurt?

BILAL
No...but she's hurtin' for you and what happened.
She's here if you want me to go and get her...

(Bilal stands and heads to the door)

TALIB
Helllllll no. PLEEEEAAASSSSEEEE STOP. Don't get her. I
don't want to see her. I don't want to see anybody else.

BILAL
OK, OK, calm down, calm down. We're done talking. It's time for you
to get some rest and relax. I'll be right here if you need anything.

(Later that evening, Craig, Angel, Hanna and Bilal wait in the lobby while
Talib sleeps. Craig and Angel fall away leaving Bilal and Hanna alone.)

BILAL
(Grudgingly, but concerned)
You, OK?

HANNA
(Slumped over and slightly numb)
I can't even think straight right now. And I can't believe
you are here so soon after Jonathan was killed…

BILAL
There is so much shit going on right now…at home…in the streets…and
now this…Jonathan is GONE…but Talib is still here so I just felt….

(Bilal gets choked up and can't finish thought)

HANNA
(Reaching out to Bilal)
No explanation needed.

BILAL
…And we did get your card and basket. My mom
sends you her thanks for your kindness.

HANNA
She's welcome…You are welcome.

(Both sit silently staring at the ground.)

BILAL
So, I heard you jumped in and fought the attackers?!…See, like I told
Talib: I knew you was crazy. What if they'd had a gun or somethin'?

HANNA
(Irate)
Listen, people just don't get to harass us, assault us, BEAT
THE SHIT OUT OF US for no gotdamn reason…
just because we are Muslim. FUCK THEM.

BILAL
(Laughing)
You know what? You got HEART! And you really did look out for my
boy…at your own expense. So, you might just be alright…for a White girl.

HANNA
Oh, so now I'm alright…since I'm willing to get
my ass beat, huh? Fuck you, Bilal.

BILAL
Hey, hey. Calm down. I don't want you whoopin' my ass here in this lobby.

(Bilal laughs and Hanna breaks into laughter as well.)

Fa' real. Seriously Hanna. I was wrong before. Before I could only
see history. Now, I see YOU. You are a real live person who put your
OWN safety on the line for another. THAT kind of courage matters.

HANNA
(Becoming serious)
Bilal, this shit IS HORRIBLE. Americans assaulting Muslim-
Americans. Muslim-Americans slaughtering fellow soldiers.
WHAT THE HELL ARE WE GOING TO DO?

BILAL
I don't know Hanna. I JUST DON'T KNOW.

(Both give each other grudging smirk and the lights go down!)

SCENE III

(Later in the week, Hanna stops by to see Talib.)

HANNA
(Peeking in the door)
Hey Talib!

TALIB
Hey Hanna. Come on in.

HANNA
Are you sure? I mean we have to be careful when
we are alone together because....

TALIB
(Giggling a bit)
Girl, come on in. Anyway, the blinds are open.

HANNA
Really, I wont stay long....

TALIB
It's OK, really. I needed to see you to say thank you.

HANNA
Oh, well, it's the least I could do. If I could have kept up
with my purse like you are always telling me then...

TALIB
Han, this isn't about your purse...or your fault.
We got attacked---end of story.

HANNA

I also wanted you to know that I GET IT. Yall have been trying to warn me, guide me, help me understand, but I've been to blind to see it...too unwilling to see things from your point of view. I'm just sick about this.

TALIB

Hanna, really, that has no bearing on what
they did. They were wrong, not you.

HANNA

Well, I'm not sure how much good its going to do with the
police?! And now word on campus is I'm a race traitor.

TALIB

Damn, Han, for real?

HANNA

That's OK, though, This isn't a popularity contest.
I HAD TO DO THE RIGHT THING!

TALIB

Hanna, I just feel bad because since you converted it's
just literally been one damn thing after another?!

HANNA

Well, you know what they say. HARD TIMES PURIFY, RIGHT?!

TALIB

(Yawns)
Whew, OK, Hanna. I'm getting sleepy.

HANNA

OK, i'll go, but I'll text you later. Salaamu Alaikum, brother Talib.

TALIB

Wa'laikum Salaam, Sister Hanna.

SCENE IV

(Lights come up again with Craig on the phone with the Dean.)

CRAIG
...But it's been two weeks...and the police don't have
ANY leads? They say the trail has gone cold? Yeah, I just
bet is has. OK, OK. Well, did you get my proposal.

(Pausing to try and calm himself)

I sent you a proposal asking you to support the establishment of a
Muslim Student Advisory Committ ee to promote awareness and
understanding between Muslim and non-Muslim students.

(Pauses to hear the Dean's responses)

What do you mean "it's not in the budget"? All I'm asking you for is
some pizza and soda money and a few dollars to compensate student
leaders for their time? Oh, you don't have any money for this, but
you just gave the Campus Knitting Club $500.00 for the semester???
And these kids are being beaten and assaulted and you can't...OK,
OK, just be ready for the lawsuit when somebody gets killed.

(Shortly after the Dean's call, Angel knocks on his door.)

ANGEL
Hey Craig. How are you?

CRAIG
Hey, girl. What brings you by?

ANGEL
Just checking on you. Been a crazy moment for you and your students.

CRAIG
(Closing folder)
Yeah, that's exactly what I'm working on pulling together
a proposal to support these students by way of a Muslim
Student Advisory Committee (MSAC).

ANGEL
Advisory Committee? Craig, these students have been
through some really traumatic events this semester.
Have any of them been through counseling?

CRAIG
Well, I've been trying to reach them to follow up, but none of
them are returning my calls. So, I'm going to stop by and see
them because I want them to be involved in MSAC. And, I want
to include Hanna, of course. By the way, how is she doing?

ANGEL
She's really distant these days. All that passion and excitement for life
has just drained out of her. Every time I try to meet with her, she gives
me some story about studying, a quiz, having to work….all legitimate
reasons, but odd. So, I think you need to be really careful with these
kids. Has any progress been made in finding their attackers?

CRAIG
No, and it's complicated as these are all students involved in this…and the
ones with the best attorneys tend to fare better than others. It also doesn't
hurt to be a member of a popular frat with powerful alumni on campus.
So, the matter get's spun as a love triangle…as opposed to a hate crime.

ANGEL
Well, for all these reason, Craig. Don't make these students the poster
children for some great cause or movement. Deal with them as the
INDIVIDUAL victims of crimes (both on and off campus) for now.

CRAIG

But Angel, that's just it. It's these incidents of hatred that can
be the cornerstone of a powerful movement against…

ANGEL
(Getting adamant)
Craig, Craig, I'm telling you. Let them heal. If you want to do something,
press law enforcement and PRESS THE INSTITUTION to address
this issue, but don't force these student to carry the water on this.

CRAIG
(Coming around his desk to approach her)
OK, Angel. We'll see. But what are you doing here, exactly. I
know you didn't stop by here to argue about students.

ANGEL
(Exasperated and feeling patronized)
I came by to SEE ABOUT YOU, but as usual
you and your students are inseparable.

CRAIG
Angel, what do you want from me?

(Their eyes lock, but her prayer reminder chirps on her
phone shaking both of them out their locked gaze.)

ANGEL
Uh, uh, nothing now. I need to go. I'll holler at you later.

CRAIG
But Angel, wait…

(End of Scene.)

(Craig appears at Bilal and Talib's room to check on them and pay his respects to Bilal for his loss. As he approaches he hears the two men talking as Bilal---no longer weating his kufi--- packs boxes and bags. Talib is still bruised from the attack.)

TALIB

B, are you SURE you want to do this? Come on, think about it, the semester is almost over?

BILAL

(Boxing up things frantically)

Bruh, you need to be right behind me. We've been over this a thousand times already. Moms is a mess and I need to get home to help out.

TALIB

So, you just gone roll out on me?!

BILAL

You need to go the fuck home, too. It ain't safe here.

TALIB

But we go to school here. Pay tuition here. Hell, our Moms and Pops pay taxes for us to be up in here just like everybody else.

BILAL

(Throwing a shirt down fiercely)

And that didn't make a damn bit of difference did it?! You still got your ass beat.

(Craig knocks.)

CRAIG

Hey, wassup fellas. I just stopped by to see how room #812 is doin'.

71

(Craig hugs Bilal, then look around room concerned)

CRAIG

Bilal, you taking a trip this weekend?

BILAL

Nah, man, I had to withdraw from school.

CRAIG

Wait, wait, wait...WHY?

TALIB

You know, his brother was killed in the Fort Hood massacre.

CRAIG

Yeah, yeah, and its terrible, but WHY WITHDRAW?

BILAL

With Jon gone, mom's needs the help at home with finances.

CRAIG

OK, but man, listen, what if we can get you a lil' job on
campus and you send some of THAT money home.

BILAL

Man, we need more than one of these lil' campus jobs wit' the bills we
got. I got a line on some legit jobs that will help us out in the short term.

TALIB

(Rolling his eyes)

Man, please, don't blame this lame-ass decision on your mom. She never
asked you to do this. She WANTS YOU TO STAY HERE and finish
your degree--- instead of taking some lousy-ass job in the 'hood.

BILAL

(Furious)

T, shut the fuck up talkin' shit to me. All the Pakistanis and Arab
shops in the hood is the reason Black folks ain't got shit now....

(Bilal throws up his hands admitting he went too far.)

OK, OK, sorry man, I'm sorry for that. It's just that while yall doin'
all this talkin', neither the university nor these beloved Muslims
ain't cut me the first check... or even sent a sympathy card from the
mosque--- but they were rolling deep to see you at the hospital...

TALIB

(Equally furious)

Yeah, the mosque staff can be lousy, but Imam Hakim did call and
asked to come by several times, but you won't call him back. B, don't
start that "Muslims-don't-give-a- shit" bit. Yeah, my pops own gas
station/convenience stores in the Black neighborhood. But he also
supports a local school in the neighborhood, donates to the library
down the street and offers scholarships to kids with good grades
every year. So you can shut up wit' all that. WE ain't all alike either.

CRAIG

(Exasperated, shouting)

Hey, hey fellas, calm down for a minute. B, can't you see
Talib cares about you and you just gon' roll out on him?

BILAL

(Shouting right back)

Man, please, he's got you and Hanna and the whole
mosque looking out for him. He'll be straight.

CRAIG

So you just gon' let the terrorists win, huh?

BILAL
What?

CRAIG
That crazy muthafucka in Texas stole your brother and now ignorant -ass
folks at the mosque and in this community gotchu' on the run.

BILAL
(Tearing up and shouting)
Man, you think I wanna leave when I had to
work so hard to get THIS far???

CRAIG
(In his face)
HELL NO, MAN! So stay here and show
them ALL that they can't beat you.
(Bilal collapses on the bed weeping covering his face with
a towel. Craig and Talib stare at one another.)

BILAL
(Lamenting with towel over his face)
I WANT MY BROTHER BACK. I WANT JONATHAN BAAAAACK.

SCENE VI

(Craig is in his office pouring over papers when Angel stops
by. She is no longer wearing her hijab or headscarf.)

ANGEL
Knock-knock.

(Craig looks up and is shocked by her and seeing her without a scarf...
and is struck by how much more attractive she is than he realized.)

CRAIG
Oh, my gosh, what's up girl? I haven't seen you in a minute.
Between exams and work, it's just been hectic.

ANGEL
(Responding a bit soberly)
Yeah, this semester has indeed been crazy. How is your student doing?

CRAIG
Great question. I've been on him to come in and meet with
me. He's been eerily quiet lately. But hold on, hold on just
wait a minute... come on now, let's just get this said.

(CRAIG waves his hands in front of his hands and face.)

You've made quite a change, Ms. Thing, WHAT'S UP??? If, if you
don't mind me asking, why aren't you covering anymore?

ANGEL
I'm scared, Craig. Everything is so crazy right now. Sisters are being
spit on, attacked, having their scarves snatched off their heads in the
streets. I just decided that it's not worth the hassle. It was hard to take it
off, but I can still be a Muslim and achieve my goals without covering.

CRAIG
And what goals are these exactly?

ANGEL
Craig, there is a human rights organization looking for attorneys
and law students to examine violations at Guantanamo,
do interviews, assess conditions, etc.,. so I applied to go
and I'm going to work in Cuba next semester.

CRAIG
Next semester? You mean, like NEXT MONTH?

ANGEL
Yep. And I'm really excited about it. It's a great opportunity to work
in human rights law, a chance to visit family in Cuba and just get
the fuck out of the United States right now. It's too hard to be here
AND be Muslim sometimes. So, by going away, I can still work for
my country and my faith at the same time. How ironic is that?

CRAIG
CAN you?

ANGEL
How are we going to get a handle on terrorism if we don't
even know what we are doing to our own "combatants"?

CRAIG
(Still in shock.)
You really are hyped up about this aren't you?

ANGEL
Yeah, I am.

CRAIG
(Sighs, a bit disappointed, but trying to hide it)
Well, I'm happy for you and I know you will have a great
experience…and a lot to share when you return.

ANGEL
(Flirtatiously)
So, do you mind if I keep in touch with you while I'm there?

(CRAIG smiled broadly.)
CRAIG
No, not at all. As a matter of fact, I'D LOVE THAT.

(Just them, TALIB knocks at CRAIG'S door. His baseball
cap has been replaced with an Islamic skullcap.

CRAIG
Well, well. Look who's here?

ANGEL
(Smiling, but regretting Talib's timing)

OK, Craig. Let me let you all chat.

CRAIG
(CRAIG stands up and coming around the desk
to discourage ANGEL from leaving)

Uh, Angel, wait, wait, can you…

ANGEL
(Angel grabbed Craig's hand for the first time.)
Don't worry. I'll find you. We'll get together before I leave.

(Turning to Talib with sincere concern.)

Assalamu Alaikum Brother Talib. How are you?

TALIB
(Shocked to see Angel without her scarf)
Hey, Sister Angelica. Wa Alaikum Salaam.
(Smiling)
You look REALLY DIFFERENT. Uh, oh, thank you so much
also for looking out for us while I was in the hospital. I got your
emails, but I hadn't seen you in person to thank you until now.

ANGEL
You are welcome, brother. I'm just glad to see you out and feeling better.

TALIB
(TALIB turns away from ANGEL.)
I am, I am, Sister Angel.

(Angel looked back at Craig, concerned, but departs.)

ANGEL
Craig, I'll call you later.

(Craig nods VERY HOPEFULLY, EXCITEDLY…
and turns his attention to Talib.)

CRAIG
Come on in and sit down. It's good to see you.

TALIB
Sorry if I ran Sister Angelica off. I should have called first.

CRAIG
Not a problem at all. How are YOU doing?

TALIB

Well, I just wanted to come by to thank you for working with all my professors to get excused absences for me so I can submit late assignments.

CRAIG

That's THE LEAST we can do. It's amazing that you went back to classes especially after Bilal withdrew for the semester. So, it must be lonely for you here. But, since you are feeling up to getting back into the swing of things, have you thought more about a declared major?

(Craig stands to get Talib's folder).

I also wanted to talk with you about a project
that I'd love for you to be a part of...

TALIB

Actually, that's what I came to talk to you about. I think I want
to take off next semester. I need a break from school.

CRAIG
(Stunned)
Aw, Talib, man. You were doing so well in your classes and...

TALIB

It's been OK, but I think I'd be better off closer to home and family.

CRAIG

I'm sure this is also more difficult now that Bilal is gone. But Talib: I NEED you to stay. I just secured funding from the Dean's Office to establish the MSAC---The Muslim Students Advocacy Committee to create support and advocacy for Muslim students on campus. And I think you will be a wonderful addition to our our Muslim Student Leadership Teams---who will offer peer counseling and program development on campus. I've also been reaching out to Bilal to try to encourage him to come back and be reinstated without a lot of red tape.

(CRAIG rises to show Talib the proposal for the project.)

TALIB
Oh, so now I'm supposed to be down with your GREAT CAUSE?!
Thanks, but NO THANKS! It sounds cool, but I think I'm just
going to take my cousin up on his offer to visit him in Pakistan.
And I really could use the break and it will be nice to hang out with
some of the brothers over there and see what they are up to.

CRAIG
(Nearly frantic)

Talib, PLEASE DON'T GO!

TALIB
Why not? I got family there?

CRAIG
I know that the anti-Muslim climate is strong, but
don't give up on your education right now.

(CRAIG points to Talib's head)

I see your dress has changed already.

TALIB
(Talib looks down)

Craig, what's the point of denying my culture.
Besides, i'm tired trying to fit in.

CRAIG
So, don't leave and hide out there. You are an AMERICAN, Talib.

TALIB

(Bitterly)

And that don't mean shit these days if folks don't believe it...or accept it?

CRAIG

Talib, all I'm saying is that you have worked too
hard... been through too much....

TALIB

Why do we have to continue to teach other folks about who we are ...and
THEN STILL BE MISTREATED. TO HELL WIT' THAT.

CRAIG

Well, what about Hanna?

TALIB

(Sucking his teeth and rolling his eyes)

What about her?

CRAIG

T, it doesn't make you any less Muslim to like
her. She really cares about you.

TALIB

I just came to school to get a degree, return home and start
my life, family, kids. I didn't expect for my best friend to fall
apart, to get my ass kicked, or to have this white girl to deal
with. Naaaaaaaah, I cain't deal wit' ANY OF IT right now.

CRAIG

I know that it's been a crazy time. But, college is like that sometimes. Some
of the shit you go through in college is fucked up... and some of it will
bless your life--- if you let it. WE NEED YOU HERE IN SCHOOL...the
Muslim community, your peers, your friends, your family. We need YOUR

compassion, YOUR intellect, YOUR fire HERE. Come on man, I need you to work with me to keep other young Muslims alive. Will you help me?

(Craig reaching out his hand to Talib. Talib sits motionless.)

(FADE TO BLACK. PLAY ENDS.)

.